Wonders of the World

Uluru

The Largest Monolith in the World

Jennifer Hurtig

www.av2books.com

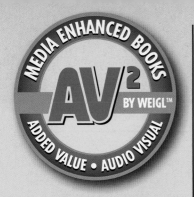

AV² provides enriched content that supplements and complements this book. Weigl's AV² books strive to create inspired learning and engage young minds in a total learning experience.

Your AV² Media Enhanced books come alive with...

Audio
Listen to sections of the book read aloud.

Key Words
Study vocabulary, and complete a matching word activity.

Video
Watch informative video clips.

Quizzes
Test your knowledge.

Go to www.av2books.com, and enter this book's unique code.

BOOK CODE

R449108

Embedded Weblinks
Gain additional information for research.

Slide Show
View images and captions, and prepare a presentation.

AV² by Weigl brings you media enhanced books that support active learning.

Try This!
Complete activities and hands-on experiments.

... and much, much more!

Published by AV² by Weigl
350 5th Avenue, 59th Floor
New York, NY 10118
Website: www.av2books.com   www.weigl.com

Library of Congress Control Number: 2013953164

ISBN 978-1-4896-0760-7 (hardcover)
ISBN 978-1-4896-0761-4 (softcover)
ISBN 978-1-4896-0762-1 (single user eBook)
ISBN 978-1-4896-0763-8 (multi-user eBook)

Printed in the United States of America in North Mankato, Minnesota
1 2 3 4 5 6 7 8 9 18 17 16 15 14

012014
WEP301113

Editor Heather Kissock
Design Mandy Christiansen

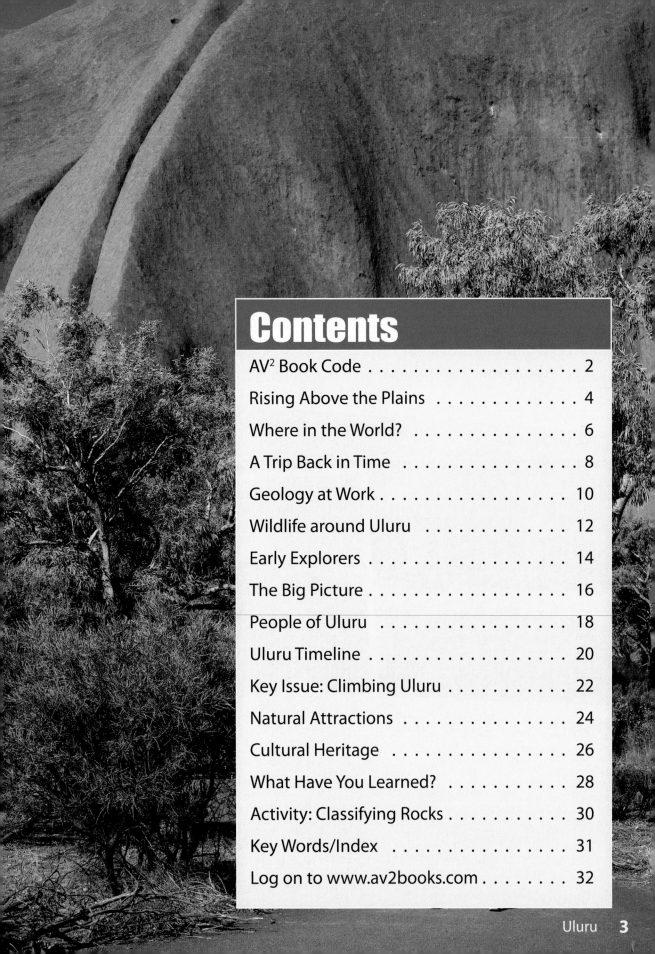

Contents

Rising Above the Plains

Uluru is a **monolith** that rises high above the plains of central Australia. It is composed of a single piece of **sandstone** rock. From far away, Uluru looks very smooth, but close up, it has many holes, caves, ribs, and valleys.

Nearby lies another rock formation, Kata Tjuta. Together, Uluru and Kata Tjuta form a national park. This park is protected as a **UNESCO World Heritage Site** because it has a strong cultural and historical value. People come to see the interesting rock formations at Uluru-Kata Tjuta and to learn about the culture of Australia's Aboriginal people. **Aboriginal Australians** have lived in Uluru for more than 30,000 years.

Both Uluru and Kata Tjuta are important ceremonial and cultural places to many Aboriginal Australians.

The Kata Tjuta mounds are also called the Olgas, after their highest peak. Mount Olga reaches a height of 1,791 feet (546 meters).

Uluru-Kata Tjuta Facts

- Uluru is the largest monolith in the world.
- Kata Tjuta means "many heads" in the local Aboriginal language.
- Uluru measures almost 5.8 miles (9.4 kilometers) around the base.
- Uluru-Kata Tjuta National Park has been named a World Heritage Site for its natural and cultural values.
- Kata Tjuta is composed of 36 rock domes that lie 26 miles (42 km) west of Uluru. They are made of a mix of pebbles, boulders, and cobbles cemented together with mud.

Map of Uluru

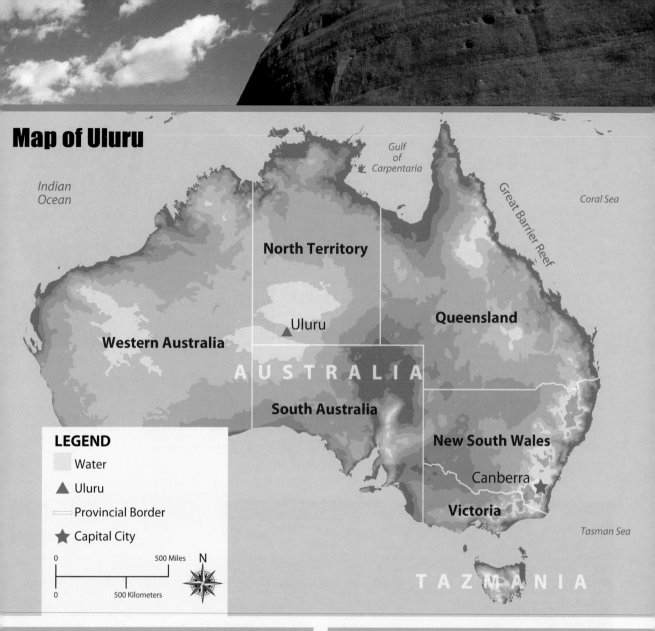

Indian
Ocean

Gulf
of
Carpentaria

Great Barrier Reef

Coral Sea

North Territory

Uluru ▲

Queensland

Western Australia

A U S T R A L I A

South Australia

New South Wales

Canberra ★

Victoria

Tasman Sea

T A Z M A N I A

LEGEND
- Water
- ▲ Uluru
- ══ Provincial Border
- ★ Capital City

| 0 | 500 Miles |
| 0 | 500 Kilometers |

N

Approximately 178 species of birds have been recorded in the park, including falcons and buzzards.

Many lizard species are found in the park, including the rare desert skink.

Where in the World?

U luru-Kata Tjuta National Park is located in the southwestern area of the Northern Territory of Australia. This central area of Australia is often called the "Red Center" because the soil is so red. This area is very dry and hot and has few towns or settlements. It is a land of deserts and mountain ranges. There are mountain ranges both to the north and south of the park.

Like the broadleaf parakeelya, many vibrant wildflowers make their homes in the arid sands of the Australian outback.

Uluru-Kata Tjuta National Park lies more than 1,000 miles (1,600 km) from any major city in Australia. The nearest large town is Alice Springs, more than 200 miles (320 km) to the northeast. Most visitors to the national park fly into Alice Springs. It is a popular winter resort for vacationers and tourists, as well as a center for mining and livestock rearing.

Alice Springs, a town of about 20,000, is considered to be the gateway to Uluru-Kata Tjuta.

Fires

Aboriginals light sections of dry grass on fire during controlled burns. This helps prevent the breakout of larger, uncontrolled bushfires during hot summer days.

Early explorers sometimes noticed that there was smoke coming from Uluru. This is because Aboriginal Australians used a tjangi, or fire stick, to burn patches of bushy spinifex grass. As the old plants burned, their nutrients would sink into the ground and help new plants to grow. Aboriginal Australians burned spinifex grass to encourage new growth of grasses that would attract animals, such as kangaroos, which they hunted for food.

Controlled fires are still lit today, mostly in winter. This helps to burn off dry grasses that could become fuel for a big fire in summer. Uncontrolled fires can do a great deal of damage. In 1976, two fires burned 76 percent of the park's plants. Another fire in 2002 burned a vast majority of the park.

A Trip Back in Time

Aboriginal Australians still live in the area around Uluru and Kata Tjuta. An Aboriginal group called Anangu are the traditional owners of Uluru. Anangu have their own creation story about Uluru. They believe that there was nothing on Earth until their **ancestors** came. Then, the ancestral creator beings formed the landscape and rocks that can be seen today. Anangu believe that they, as well as the plants and animals that live around them, are descended from these ancestral spirits.

Anangu explanations about how Uluru developed are different from those of geologists. Geologists believe that the rock that makes up Uluru formed about 550 million years ago during the **Cambrian period.**

Aboriginal Australians have inhabited the Uluru area for at least 22,000 years.

Caves

Ikari is also called the "smile cave" because of its mouth-like appearance.

Along the edges of Uluru and Kata Tjuta are shallow caves. These caves provided Anangu people with shelter from harsh weather. The Aboriginal Australians also held sacred ceremonies here and drew paintings on the walls of the caves.

Ikari is a cave on the southeastern side of Uluru. It contains very old animal bones and teeth. These bones are hundreds of years old. They came from animals that once lived in Uluru or were carried into the cave by other animals, such as owls.

The name of this cave comes from an Anangu story of a Willy Wagtail woman called Ikari, who once lived in the cave. A Willy Wagtail is a small bird found in Australia.

Geology at Work

During the Cambrian period, there were violent movements of the Earth's **crust**. Molten, or liquid, rock reached the surface and created a range of mountains made of **granite**. Over the next 50 million years, the mountains **eroded**. This process created thick layers of **sediment** over a wide area. Earth's crust again shifted dramatically about 310 to 340 million years ago. This shifting made the layers of sediment tilt.

Today, the layers can be seen as ridges on the sides of Uluru. Weathering by wind and water have given Uluru its unique shape. Only the top of the Uluru rock is visible. Much of it lies underground. Scientists estimate that Uluru may extend 3.6 miles (5.8 km) underground.

To the Anangu people, the ribs, ridges and caves of Uluru represent voyages and activities of their ancestral beings.

The Importance of Water

The valleys and gorges of Kata Tjuta provide protection for the many plants and animals found there.

There are many valleys and **gorges** in Uluru-Kata Tjuta. Rainstorms formed these gorges over millions of years. Water flowing down the rocks created large grooves where valleys are today.

Water is very important to the people who live in this desert. The average yearly rainfall in this area is less than 9 inches (23 centimeters). Rainwater is quickly absorbed into the ground.

Despite this, there usually is water around the base of Uluru. When it rains, the water runs down the rock and collects in pools. Water also can be found in the layers of sand in a valley between Uluru and Kata Tjuta. This water eventually drains into Lake Amadeus, a few miles (km) to the north.

Wildlife around Uluru

The area around Uluru is full of wildlife. More than 20 species of mammals live there. Some small mammals, such as mulgaras and moles, live in burrows and tunnels in the sand. Bats live in caves and cracks in the rocks. Larger mammals, such as red kangaroos, dingoes, and wallaroos, also live around Uluru. Camels, foxes, cats, dogs, and rabbits have been brought to Australia from other countries. They are causing great harm to the natural environment.

Besides its distinctive thorns, the thorny devil also has the ability to change color so that it blends in with its environment.

Reptiles, such as pythons and skinks, and amphibians, such as frogs, thrive in this region. Some bird species live near Uluru all year long, but others only arrive after there has been rain. Anangu name birds for their calls. They use the name *piyar-piyarpa* for galahs or *walawuru* for wedgetail eagles.

Dingoes, or Australian wild dogs, are Australia's largest meat-eating mammals. Their diet consists mainly of rabbits, rodents, birds, and lizards.

Plants

More than 400 types of plants and vegetation grow in and around Uluru. Plants that grow in the Uluru area must adapt to the hot, dry conditions. The mulga is a common tree in Australia. This tree has developed a survival strategy to deal with bush fires. Its seeds require heat to crack and **germinate**.

Trees are an important resource for both people and animals. Their wood is used as firewood. Their leafy branches provide shelter for kangaroos, finch nests, and mistletoe fruit.

Shrubs, such as corkwood trees or crimson turkey bush, provide Anangu with sweet nectar. Grasses are dry and somewhat prickly. Many flowers bloom in the dry desert only after rainfall. Poisonous fruit also grow in this area. Aboriginal Australians know which fruit can be eaten.

The Anangu people use plants for purposes other than food. The bark from a corkwood tree can be used to treat burns.

Early Explorers

The first humans arrived in Australia around 60,000 years ago. They were the ancestors of today's Aboriginal Australians. These people knew about Uluru for tens of thousands of years before the first European discovered the enormous rock. The first person of European descent to see Uluru was Ernest Giles in October, 1872. He saw it from far away and described it as "the remarkable pebble."

On July 19, 1873, William Gosse, a surveyor who was mapping unknown areas of Australia, arrived at Uluru and named it Ayers Rock. It was named after Sir Henry Ayers, the chief secretary of South Australia. Many tourists and miners had come to Uluru by the 1950s. The Australian government established Uluru, Kata Tjuta, and the surrounding land as a national park in 1958.

English explorer Ernest Giles published several volumes detailing his exploration of the Australian continent between the years of 1861 and 1875.

Biography

William Gosse (1842–1881)

In 1873, explorer and surveyor William Christie Gosse became the first non-Aboriginal person to reach Uluru. He worked for the surveyor-general's office and had already surveyed the far northern and southeastern districts of South Australia.

After those explorations, the government sent Gosse to explore more of South Australia. Gosse was looking to find a route between Alice Springs and Perth, on Australia's southwestern coast, when he reached Uluru. He and his team of men had to turn back before they reached Perth, but they mapped more than 60,000 square miles (155,000 sq km) of previously uncharted land.

AUSTRALIA 18c

W GOSSE

An Australian postage stamp was issued in 1976 to commemorate William Gosse's discovery of Uluru in 1873.

The Big Picture

A monolith is a single massive rock or stone. Uluru is just one of many monoliths located in Australia. There are many other monoliths around the world, too. Some of these include El Capitan in the United States, Zuma Rock in Nigeria, and Sugarloaf Mountain in Brazil.

Sugarloaf Mountain
Brazil

Devils Tower
United States

NORTH AMERICA

PACIFIC OCEAN

ATLAN OCE

EQUATOR

SOUTH AMERICA

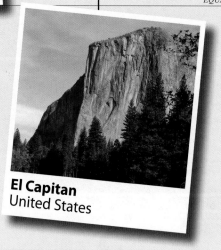

El Capitan
United States

LEGEND

 Ocean

River

Scale at Equator

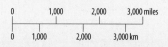

0   1,000   2,000   3,000 miles

0   1,000   2,000   3,000 km

N

SOUTHER OCEAN

Zuma Rock
Nigeria

Sigiriya
Sri Lanka

Uluru
Australia

ARCTIC OCEAN

ASIA

EUROPE

AFRICA

EQUATOR

INDIAN
OCEAN

AUSTRALIA

SOUTHERN
OCEAN

ANTARCTICA

People of Uluru

At one time, Anangu people moved around to hunt and to find food. Some Anangu today still live off the land's resources. They gather wild fruits, seeds, and vegetables, and hunt animals for food, including kangaroos, lizards, and birds.

Many Anangu have combined their traditional culture with modern conveniences. About 300 Anangu live near Uluru in the community of Mutitjulu. Many work in the park alongside park rangers, sharing their knowledge of the area with the rangers and visitors. They lead tours of the site and teach people how to live in the hot, dry climate.

Aboriginal park guides share traditional tales of Uluru and their people with groups of visitors on the Anangu Cultural Tour at Uluru-Kata Tjuta National Park.

Anangu Beliefs

Anangu elders pass down their stories and traditions to the younger generations in order to keep their culture alive.

The basis of Anangu knowledge is called *Tjukurpa*. The word *Wapar* is used to describe Anangu laws and beliefs. These two words involve many concepts. They include history, the present, and the future. These words also describe the way people, plants, animals, and the land interact, as well as the knowledge of how these relationships came to be.

Tjukurpa is passed on through oral storytelling. It is not written in books. To help Anangu remember Tjukurpa, they have created songs, dances, and art. Stories often are passed on during ceremonies. Certain people maintain their own sections of Tjukurpa. Some stories are known only by women, and other stories are just for men.

Uluru Timeline

Prehistoric

4–5 billion years ago
Earth forms.

550 million years ago
Land forms that is now Uluru.

310–340 million years ago Earth's crust shifts dramatically, and the layers of sediment that are now Uluru tilt.

65 million years ago
Dinosaurs become extinct.

50 million years ago
Australia separates from the other continents.

60,000 years ago
Ancestors of Aboriginal Australians begin living in Australia.

30,000 years ago
Windswept sands cover the plains surrounding Uluru.

Early Explorers

1770 James Cook claims Australia for Great Britain.

1872 Explorer Ernest Giles sees the rock from far away.

1873 European explorer William Gosse is the first European to discover Uluru and explore the surrounding area.

Development

1958 Uluru, Kata-Tjuta, and the surrounding area are established as a national park.

1976 A chain handhold is put on Uluru.

1978–1985 Officers of Northern Territory's Parks and Wildlife Service run the park.

1985 Uluru is given back to Anangu.

1987 Uluru-Kata Tjuta National Park is designated a UNESCO World Heritage Site for its natural and cultural value.

1993 Uluru is renamed Ayers Rock/Uluru to incorporate both the English and traditional Aboriginal names for the rock.

2000 The opening ceremonies for the 2000 Summer Olympics are held at Uluru-Kata Tjuta National Park.

2002 The order of the names is reversed to Uluru/Ayers Rock.

2002 Wildfires burn much of Uluru-Kata Tjuta National Park.

2003 A luxury accommodation at Ayers Rock Resort is destroyed by wildfires in October.

2005 Rowan Foley is appointed as the first-ever indigenous park manager at Uluru-Kata Tjuta National Park.

Present

2010 The Anangu celebrate the 25th anniversary of regaining possession of Uluru.

2010 The Australian government approves a plan to permanently close the Uluru climb portion of the park when the proportion of visitors who climb Uluru dips below 20 percent.

2013 The proportion of visitors who climb Uluru dips below 20 percent, but the climb remains open.

Climbing Uluru

Many people are fascinated by Uluru and want to climb the large rock. However, Uluru is sacred to the Anangu, so they do not climb its landscape. Anangu believe that visitors should respect their rules as they are guests on Anangu land. In 1983, the prime minister of Australia, Bob Hawke, promised to ban climbing of the rock, but this did not happen.

Climbing Uluru is a popular activity. In 1976, a chain handhold was put on the rock to give people something to hold onto while climbing. The climb up Uluru is long and steep, and, almost every year, people die attempting to climb the rock. Most deaths are caused by heart attacks or heart failure.

Despite the wishes of the Anangu, about 50,000 people attempt to climb Uluru each year. More than 40 people have died attempting to climb its steep inclines.

Anangu also do not want people to photograph the areas of Uluru where their ceremonies take place. Some areas of Uluru are only to be seen by men. Other parts of the giant rock are only to be seen by women. Anangu fear that visitors might take photographs in these areas. It would then be possible for Anangu to see pictures of forbidden places. Signs have now been put up in these places to prevent visitors from taking photographs of these sacred sites.

Should people be allowed to climb the rock?

Yes

As long as tourists are respectful of the land, they should be allowed to climb Uluru.

Tourists travel great distances to climb Uluru, and much money is raised through the tourism industry.

No

Uluru is a spiritual place for the Anangu, and tourists should respect Anangu sensitivity towards climbing the rock.

The climb can be extremely dangerous. The chain used to guide people who climb the rock stops halfway to the top. Some people have fallen to their deaths making the climb.

Natural Attractions

Despite its remoteness, hundreds of thousands of visitors make the trip to Uluru each year. The cultural center in the park has displays and exhibits about the Anangu way of life. People also enjoy walking through the valleys. The main walking trails are the Valley of the Winds and the Olga Gorge.

Depending on the time of day, Uluru seems to be different colors. This is because ash, dust particles, and **water vapor** in the **atmosphere** filter or remove some of the blue light from the Sun's rays. This means that more red light reaches the rocks than blue light. The atmosphere is not very thick around midday, but in the mornings and evenings, the atmosphere is thicker, so the light is more filtered. At these times, the sunlight reaching the rocks is mainly from the red end of the **spectrum**.

Uluru's impressive, rusty orange-red color originates from the iron content on its surfaces.

Be Prepared

When hiking through Uluru-Kata Tjuta, you must plan what to wear and what to bring because it can be very hot or windy. The clothes you bring depend on the season of your visit.

If you are traveling in the summer months, it can be very dry and hot. Make sure you wear comfortable shoes, a hat, and sunscreen. Your clothing should be light, such as shorts and a t-shirt.

In the cooler months, it can get cold at night. From August to November, it is very windy in this area. Make sure you wear more than one layer of clothing. You may want to wear warmer clothes, such as a heavy jacket and long pants.

Make sure that you drink plenty of water so that you do not become dehydrated, or dried out. Dehydration is a huge problem in the desert.

Cultural Heritage

Uluru is a sacred and important site for many Aboriginal Australians. Sacred ceremonies and storytellings about ancestors take place at Uluru. Aboriginal Australians have marked the rocks with drawings, paintings, carvings, and engravings.

Many of the landscapes have meaning to Anangu. They represent creation stories and knowledge that have been passed down for generations. Anangu beliefs discourage changes to the land.

The Australian government now protects certain Aboriginal Australian sacred sites, such as Uluru. In 1993, Ayers Rock was renamed Ayers Rock/Uluru to combine both the English and traditional Aboriginal names for the rock. Then in 2002, the order of the names was reversed to Uluru/Ayers Rock.

Uluru-Kata Tjuta National Park has preserved the Anangu people's cave paintings for viewing. These paintings represent generations of Anangu culture.

Anangu living around Uluru used art to pass on stories. They painted on cave walls and drew pictures in the sand. They also painted their bodies. Their designs told stories and had religious and ceremonial meaning. The Anangu still create works of art, but they no longer paint on the rocks.

Q: Why did Anangu use artwork to tell stories?

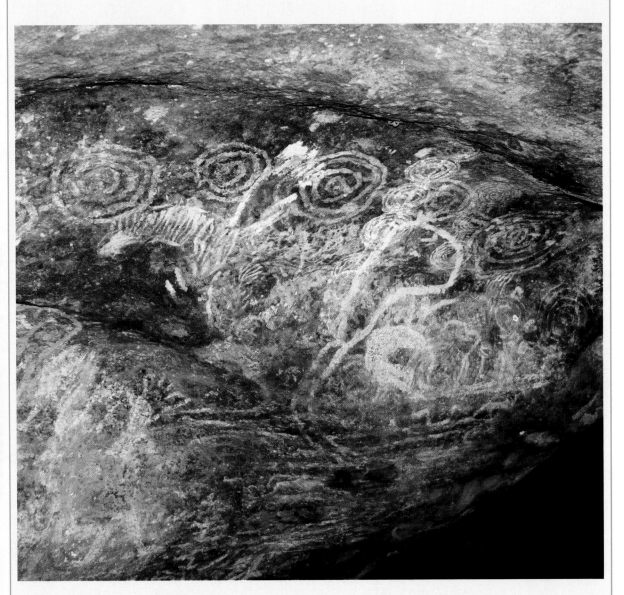

A: The Anangu created works of art to pass on stories from one generation to the next, and in this way, the stories were preserved.

True or False?

Decide whether the following statements are true or false. If the statement is false, make it true.

1. Uluru is a sacred place to Anangu.

2. Uluru-Kata Tjuta stays warm year round.

3. No plants grow here because fires burn them.

4. "Willy Wagtail" is a kind of rabbit.

5. Kata Tjuta means "many heads."

6. Anangu no longer use the natural resources of the land anymore.

ANSWERS

1. True.
2. False. Winters are cooler with strong winds. Temperatures can fall below freezing.
3. False. Some plants rely on fire to reproduce. Other plants become resistant to fire to survive.
4. False. Willy Wagtail is the name for a small Australian bird.
5. True.
6. False. Some Anangu continue to hunt for game or collect plants for food or medicine.

Short Answer

Answer the following questions using information from the book.

1. What is the name of Anangu's basis of knowledge and beliefs?

2. When did Uluru form?

3. Why did the name of Ayers Rock change to Uluru/Ayers Rock?

4. Why should people not climb Uluru?

5. Is there much water near Uluru year round?

Multiple Choice

Choose the best answer for the following questions.

1. What color does Uluru sometimes appear?
   a. green
   b. yellow
   c. red
   d. blue

2. Where in Australia is Uluru-Kata Tjuta National Park located?
   a. Southern Australia
   b. Northern Territory
   c. Queensland
   d. New South Wales

3. Which of these mammals is not native to Uluru?
   a. camel
   b. mulgara
   c. bat
   d. kangaroo

4. How many rock domes is Kata Tjuta composed of?
   a. 5
   b. 16
   c. 36
   d. 45

Activity

Classifying Rocks

Much of Earth is made up of rock. Uluru, for instance, is made up of sandstone. Geologists use special methods to classify rocks. This exercise will help you learn more about the rocks in your neighborhood.

Materials

Rocks

Glue

A box

Instructions

1. Take a walk around your house and neighborhood. Collect any interesting rocks that you find. Try to find one igneous rock, one metamorphic rock, and one sedimentary rock. Here are some features to look for.

   • Igneous rocks have small particles that look like crystals.

   • Metamorphic rocks feature lines of mineral grains that look like rocky stripes.

   • Sedimentary rocks feel sandy to touch.

2. Take your rocks home with you. Use books or online sources to identify the type of rocks you have found.

3. Prepare a box that has a place for every type of rock you found. Create a label for each type of rock.

4. Glue each rock to the box. Be sure to place each rock near its label.

5. Prepare a list of features that helped you identify each rock.

Key Words

Aboriginal Australians: the descendants of the earliest-known peoples in Australia

ancestors: people from whom a modern person is descended

atmosphere: the mass of air surrounding Earth

Cambrian period: a period in time between 550 million and 505 million years ago

crust: the rocky, outer layer of Earth

eroded: worn away, or ground down

germinate: to begin to grow, or sprout

gorges: narrow and deep passages that cut through rock

granite: a very hard variety of rock often used in buildings and monuments

monolith: a geological feature consisting of a single massive stone or rock

sandstone: a sedimentary rock formed by the compaction of sand, held together by a natural cement

sediment: sand or silt gradually deposited by wind or water and compacted to become hard

spectrum: a continuous range of colors made of different wavelengths of light

UNESCO World Heritage Site: a place that is of natural or cultural importance to the entire world. UNESCO is an abbreviation for United Nations Educational, Scientific and Cultural Organization.

water vapor: barely visible water, suspended in the air as a gas

Index

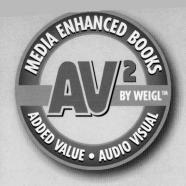

Log on to www.av2books.com

AV² by Weigl brings you media enhanced books that support active learning. Go to www.av2books.com, and enter the special code found on page 2 of this book. You will gain access to enriched and enhanced content that supplements and complements this book. Content includes video, audio, weblinks, quizzes, a slide show, and activities.

AV² Online Navigation

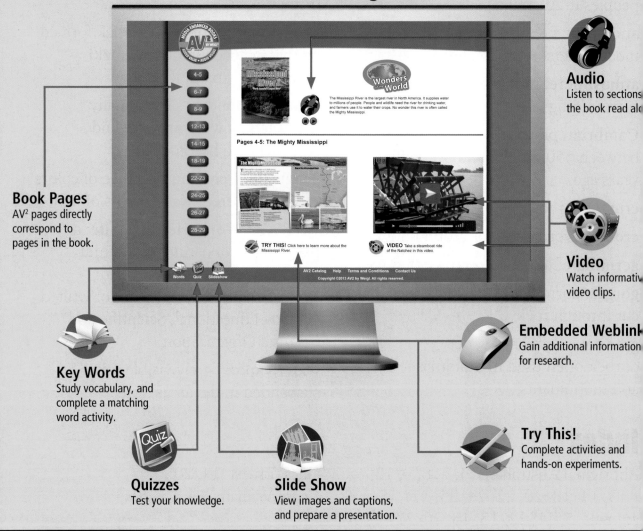

Audio
Listen to sections the book read alo

Video
Watch informativ video clips.

Book Pages
AV² pages directly correspond to pages in the book.

Embedded Weblink
Gain additional information for research.

Key Words
Study vocabulary, and complete a matching word activity.

Try This!
Complete activities and hands-on experiments.

Quizzes
Test your knowledge.

Slide Show
View images and captions, and prepare a presentation.

AV² was built to bridge the gap between print and digital. We encourage you to tell us what you like and what you want to see in the future.

Sign up to be an AV² Ambassador at www.av2books.com/ambassador.